ACOUSTIC CLASSICS
for Ukulele

ISBN 978-1-4803-5512-5

HAL•LEONARD® CORPORATION
7777 W. BLUEMOUND RD. P.O. BOX 13819 MILWAUKEE, WI 53213

Visit Hal Leonard Online at
www.halleonard.com

CONTENTS

Across the Universe

Words and Music by John Lennon and Paul McCartney

Noth - ing's gon - na change my world. _____

F   C

Noth - ing's gon - na change my world. _____

G7

Noth - ing's gon - na change my world. _____

F   C   *To Coda* ⊕

Noth - ing's gon - na change my world. _____

Verse

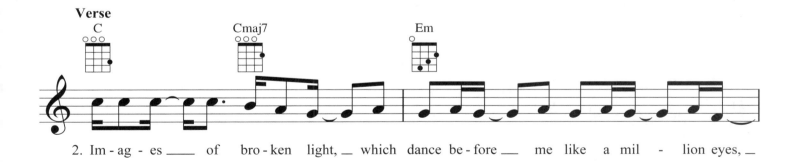

C   Cmaj7   Em

2. Im - ag - es ____ of bro - ken light, _ which dance be - fore ____ me like a mil - lion eyes, _

Dm7   G7

____ they call me on and on ____ a - cross ____ the u - ni - verse. _

Thoughts me-an - der like a rest - less wind in - side a let-ter box. __ They

D.S. al Coda

tum-ble blind - ly as they make their way a - cross __ the u - ni - verse. __

Coda
Verse

3. Sounds of laugh - ter, shades of earth __ are

ring - ing through my o - pened ears, __ in - cit - ing and in -

vit - ing me. __ Lim - it - less, __ un - dy - ing love, __ which

shines a - round __ me like a mil - lion suns, and calls me on and on __ a - cross __

Behind Blue Eyes

Words and Music by Peter Townshend

First note

Verse
Moderately

1. No one knows __ what it's like _____ to be the
2. No one knows __ what it's like _____ to feel these

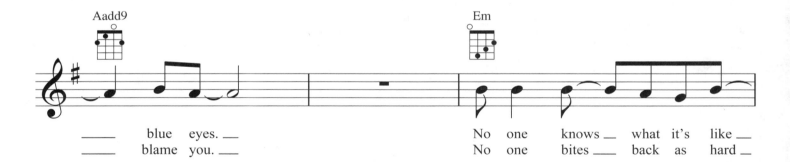

bad man, __ to be the sad man __ be - hind _
feel - ings __ like I __ do, and I _____

_____ blue eyes. __ No one knows __ what it's like __
_____ blame you. __ No one bites __ back as hard __

_____ to be hat - ed, _____ to be fat - ed _____
on their an - ger. __ None of my pain and woe

Chorus

- ger down __ my throat. And if I shiv - er, please give me a

blan - ket. Keep me warm; __ let me wear your coat. ___

Outro-Verse

No one knows __ what it's like ____ to be the

bad man, __ to be the sad man __

be - hind ____ blue eyes. __

11

Best of My Love

Words and Music by John David Souther, Don Henley and Glenn Frey

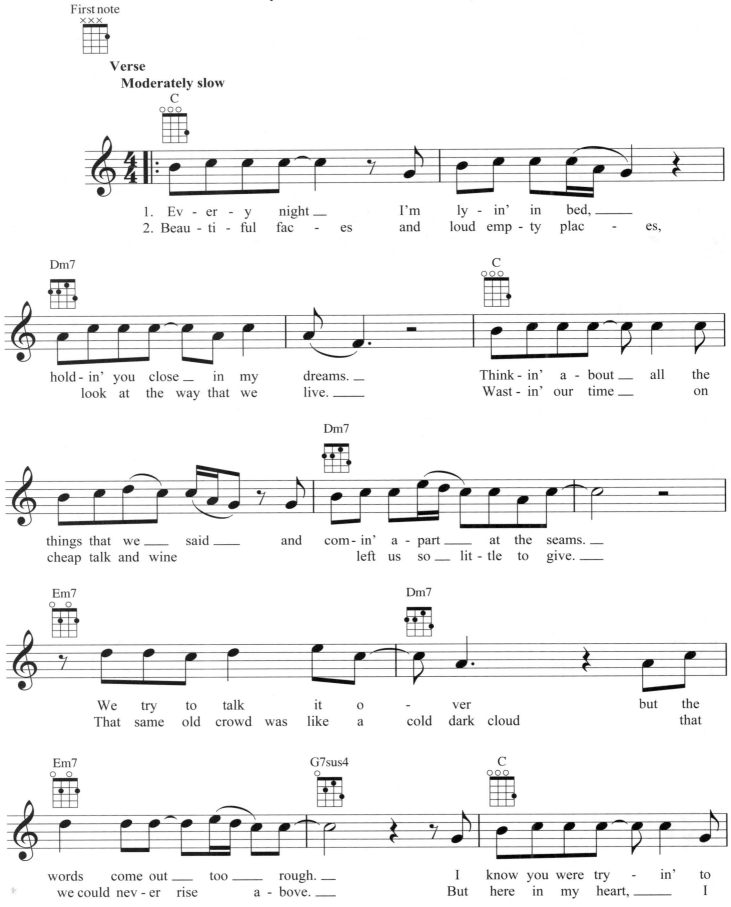

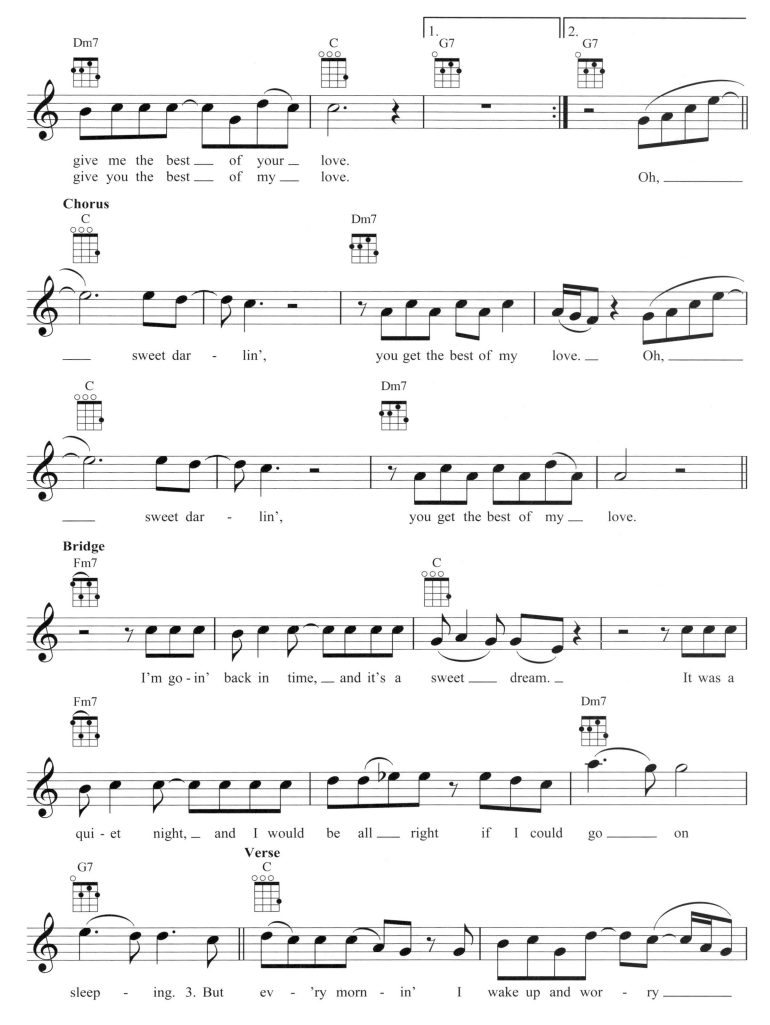

give me the best ___ of your ___ love.
give you the best ___ of my ___ love.
Oh, _____

Chorus

___ sweet dar - lin', you get the best of my love. ___ Oh, _____

___ sweet dar - lin', you get the best of my ___ love.

Bridge

I'm go - in' back in time, ___ and it's a sweet ___ dream. ___ It was a

qui - et night, ___ and I would be all ___ right if I could go ___ on

Verse

sleep - ing. 3. But ev - 'ry morn - in' I wake up and wor - ry _____

Black Water

Words and Music by Patrick Simmons

-in'. Black wa - ter keeps roll - in' on past ____

Chorus

____ just the same. _____ Old black wa - ter,

keep on roll - in'. Mis - sis - sip - pi moon, won't you

Old black wa - ter,

keep on shin - in' on me?

keep on roll - in'. Mis - sis - sip - pi moon, won't you

Old black wa - ter,

keep on shin - in' on me?

To Coda

Can't Find My Way Home

Words and Music by Steve Winwood

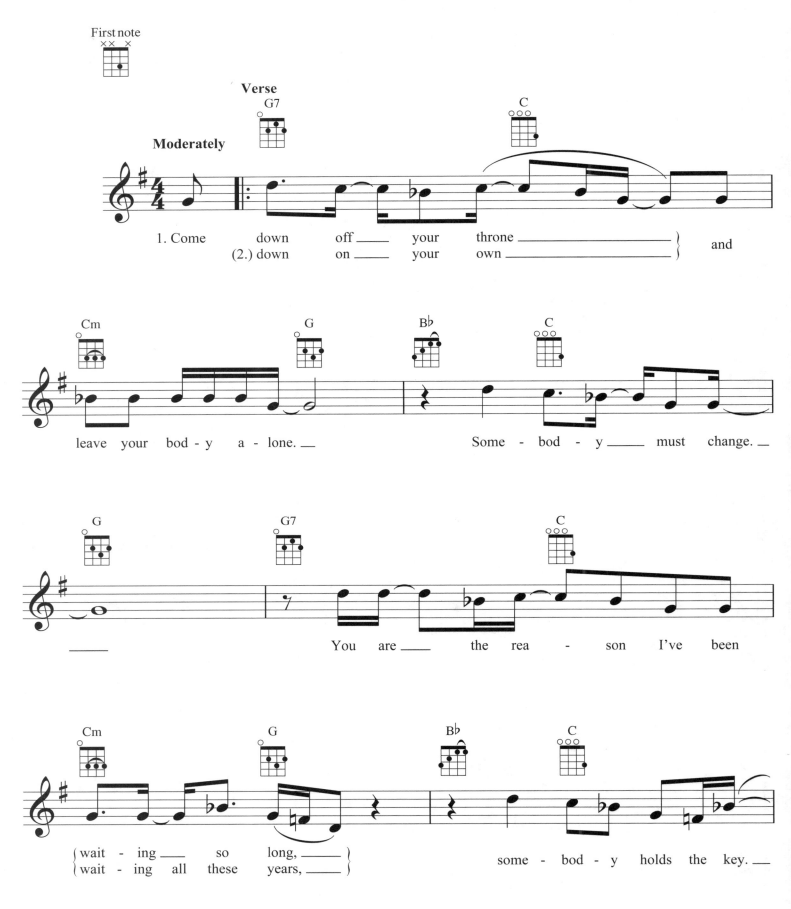

1. Come down off your throne and
(2.) down on your own

leave your bod-y a-lone. Some-bod-y must change.

You are the rea-son I've been

{ wait-ing so long, }
{ wait-ing all these years, } some-bod-y holds the key.

Cat's in the Cradle

Words and Music by Harry Chapin and Sandy Chapin

Verse
Moderate Folk style, in 2

1. My child ar - rived __ just the oth - er day; he
2., 3. *See additional lyrics*

came to the world in the u - su - al way. __ But there were planes to catch __ and

bills to pay; __ he learned to walk while I was a - way. And he was

talk - in' 'fore I knew it, and as he grew he'd say, "I'm gon - na be like

Verse

4. I've long since re-tired, my son's moved a-way; I called him up just the oth-er day. I said,"I'd like to see ___ you if you don't mind." ___ He said, "I'd love to, Dad, ___ if I can find the time. ___ You see, my new job's a has-sle and the kids have the flu, ___ but it's sure nice talk-in' to you, Dad. It's been sure nice talk-in' to you." And as I hung up the phone, it oc-

Outro-Chorus

curred to me: — he'd grown up just like me. My
boy was just like me. And the cat's in the cra-dle and the
sil - ver spoon, — lit - tle boy blue and the man — in the moon. —
"When you com - in' home, Son?" "I don't know when, but we'll get to - geth - er then, —
rit.
— Dad. — We're gon - na have a good time then."

Additional Lyrics

2. My son turned ten just the other day;
   He said, "Thanks for the ball, Dad. Come on, let's play.
   Can you teach me to throw?"
   I said, "Not today, I got a lot to do."
   He said, "That's okay." And he, he walked away,
   But his smile never dimmed, it said,
   "I'm gonna be like him, yeah.
   You know I'm gonna be like him."

3. Well, he came from college just the other day;
   So much like a man I just had to say,
   "Son, I'm proud of you. Can you sit for a while?"
   He shook his head and he said with a smile,
   "What I'd really like, Dad, is to borrow the car keys.
   See you later; can I have them, please?"

Cecilia

Words and Music by Paul Simon

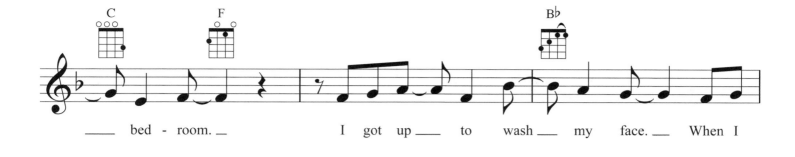

____ bed - room. ___ I got up ___ to wash ___ my face. ___ When I_

D.C. al Coda

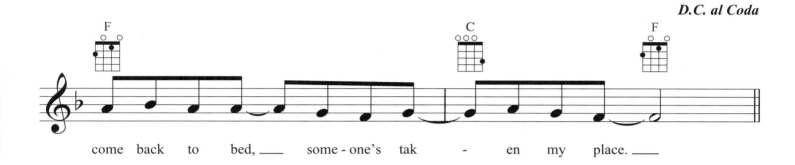

come back to bed, ___ some - one's tak - en my place. ___

Coda

___ Come on home. ___ Oh oh

Bridge

oh oh ___ oh oh oh oh oh oh oh oh ___

Outro

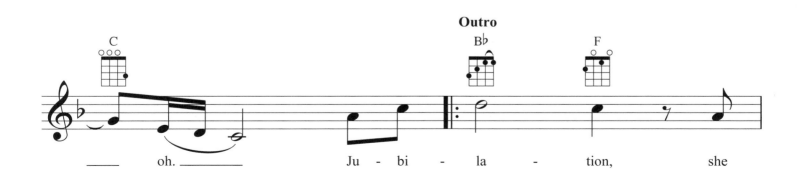

___ oh. ___ Ju - bi - la - tion, she

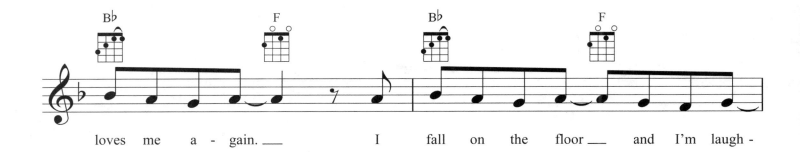

loves me a - gain. ___ I fall on the floor ___ and I'm laugh -

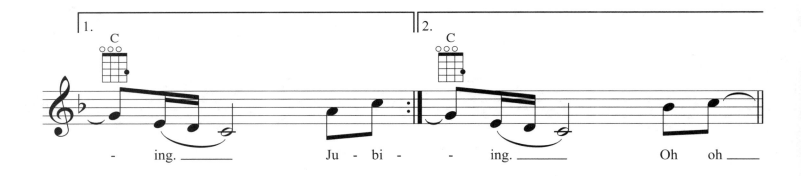

1. - ing. _____ Ju - bi - ing. _____

2. Oh oh ___

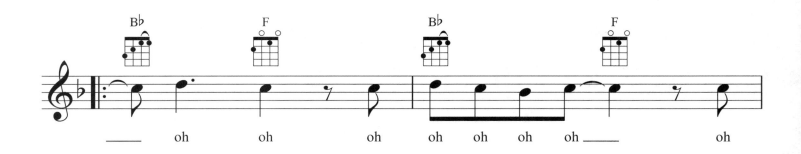

___ oh oh oh oh oh oh oh ___ oh

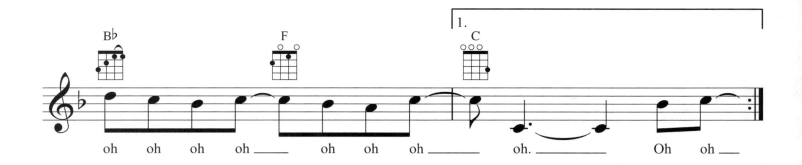

oh oh oh oh ___ oh oh oh oh. _____ Oh oh ___

1.

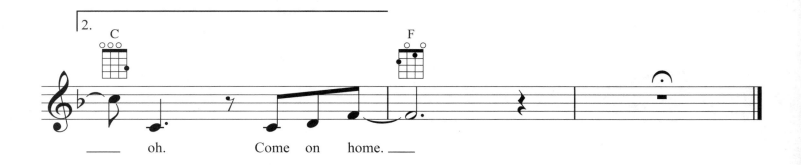

2. ___ oh. Come on home. ___

I Need You

Words and Music by Gerry Beckley

Verse
Moderately slow

1. We used to laugh, __ we used to cry, __
2. *See additional lyrics*

we used to bow __ our heads, __ then won - der why. __ But

now you're gone; __ I guess I'll car - ry on,

and make the best __ of what you've left to me, __

Additional Lyrics

2. And ev'ry day I'd laugh the hours away,
Just knowing you were thinking of me.
And then it comes, that I was put to blame
For ev'ry story told about me,
About me, about me.

Give a Little Bit

Words and Music by Rick Davies and Roger Hodgson

1. Give a lit-tle bit, _____ give a lit-tle bit __ of your love _
2., 3. *See additional lyrics*

____ to __ me. I'll give a lit-tle bit, _____

I'll give a lit-tle bit __ of my love ___ to __ you.

There's so much ___ that we need _____ to share, ___ so

send a smile ___ and show _____ you care. ___

find your-self; __ we're on _____ our way __ back home. __

Outro

__ Oh, go - in' home. __

Don't you need, don't you need to feel __ at home? __

Oh, yeah, __ we got - ta sing. __

Additional Lyrics

2. I'll give a little bit,
   I'll give a little bit of my life for you.
   So give a little bit,
   Oh, give a little bit of your time to me.
   See the man with the lonely eyes?
   Oh, take his hand; you'll be surprised.

3. Give a little bit,
   Give a little bit of your love to me.
   I'll give a little bit,
   I'll give a little bit of my life for you.
   Now's the time that we need to share,
   So find yourself; we're on our way back home.

Jack and Diane

Words and Music by John Mellencamp

Interlude

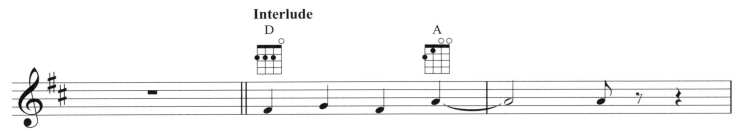

(Instrumental)

Verse

2. Suck - in' on a chil - li dog out -
3. Jack - y sits back, col - lects his

side the Tast - ee Freez. _____ Di - ane's sit - tin' on
thoughts for a _____ mo - ment, scratch - es his

Jack - y's lap; ___ he's got his hands be - tween ___ her knees.
head and does ___ his best James ___ Dean:

Jack - y say, "Hey, Di - ane, let's run off be -
"Well, then, there, Di - ane, we ought - a

hind the shad - y trees. _____
run off to ___ the cit - y."

Drib - ble off those
Di - ane says,

Bob - bie Brooks; let me do what I please."
"Ba - by, you ain't miss - in' a thing."

Chorus

Say - in': }
But Jack - y say: }

Oh yeah, _____

life goes on, _____

long af - ter the

thrill of liv - in' is ___ gone.

Say - in':

oh   yeah, _____   life _____ goes   on, _____

_____   long af - ter the   thrill   of

To Coda ⊕ | 1.   **Interlude**

liv - in' is _____ gone.   They walk   on.   *(Instrumental)*

Gon-na let it rock,

let it roll. _____

Let the Bi - ble Belt come and save my soul. __

_____ Hold on to six - teen as

long as you can. _____ Chang - es com - in' 'round

real soon make us wom - en and men.

Drums only (chords implied by vocal harmony)

4. A lit - tle dit - ty a - bout Jack and Di - ane, _____ two A - mer - i - can kids do - in' the best that they ___ can. *(Instrumental)*

Leader of the Band

Words and Music by Dan Fogelberg

to im - i - tate the man. ____ I'm just a liv - ing leg -

- a - cy ____ to the lead - er of ____ the band.

Verse

3. My broth - ers' lives were dif - f'rent, ____ for they
4. I thank you for the mu - sic ____ and your

heard an - oth - er call. ____ One went to Chi - ca -
sto - ries of the road. ____ I thank you for the free -

- go ____ and the oth - er to St. Paul. ____
- dom ____ when it came my time to go. ____

And I'm in Col - o - ra - do ____ when I'm
I thank you for the kind - ness ____ and the

42

Midnight Rider

Words and Music by Gregg Allman and Robert Kim Payne

Chorus

not gon' let 'em catch ___ me, no,   not gon' let 'em catch ___

___ the mid - night rid - er. ___   2. And I don't

D.S. al Coda   3. And I'm gone

Coda

Outro-Chorus

No, I'm not gon' let 'em catch ___ me, no,

not gon' let 'em catch ___ the mid - night rid - er. ___

Repeat and fade

___   No, I'm

Night Moves

Words and Music by Bob Seger

Out past the corn - fields where the woods __ got heav - y,

out in the back seat of my Six - ty Chev - y,

work - in' __ on mys - t'ries with - out __ an - y clues. __

Chorus

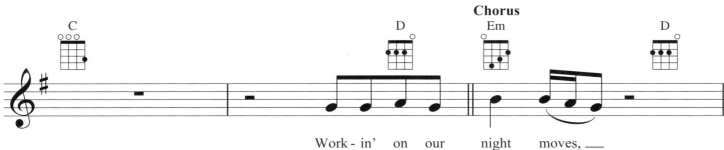

Work - in' on our night moves, __

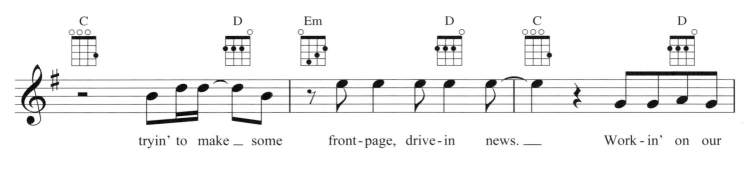

tryin' to make __ some front - page, drive - in news. __ Work - in' on our

night moves in the sum - mer - time, __

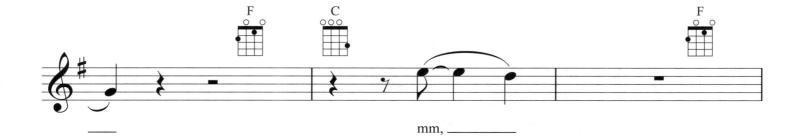

_mm, ___

in the sweet ___ sum-mer-time. _____

Verse

2. We weren't in love. Oh, no, far from it.

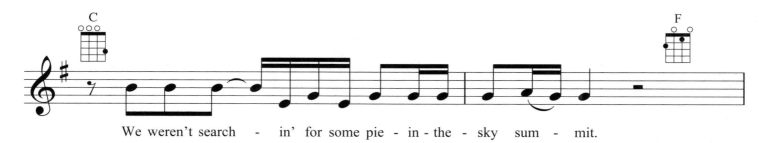

We weren't search - in' for some pie - in - the - sky sum - mit.

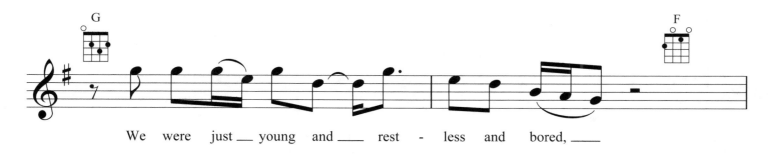

We were just ___ young and ___ rest - less and bored, ___

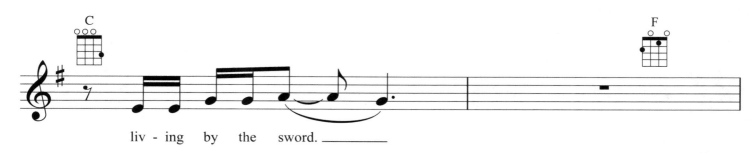

liv - ing by the sword. _____

And we'd steal a - way ev - 'ry chance we could

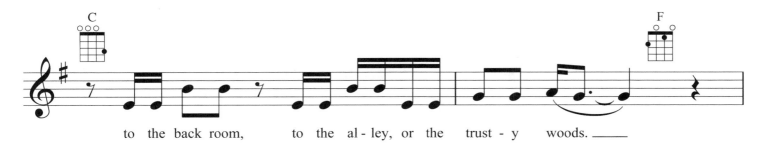

to the back room, to the al - ley, or the trust - y woods. _____

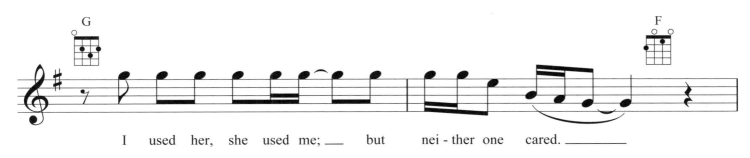

I used her, she used me; ___ but nei - ther one cared. _____

Chorus

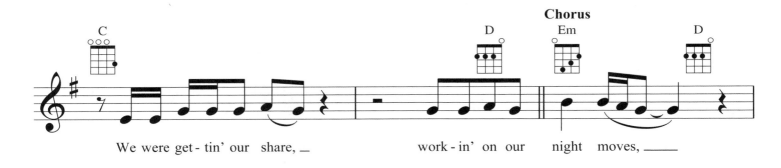

We were get - tin' our share, ___ work - in' on our night moves, _____

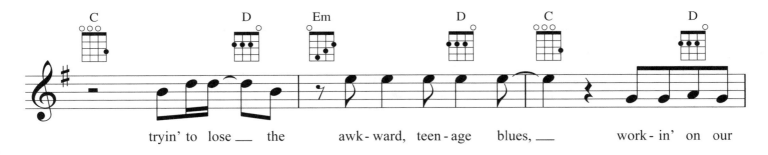

tryin' to lose ___ the awk - ward, teen - age blues, ___ work - in' on our

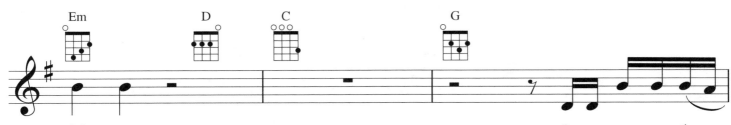

night moves. It was sum - mer - time, ___

mm, _____ sweet _

sum - mer - time, sum - mer - time. And

Bridge

oh, _____ the won - der. _____

We felt the light - ning. Yeah, _

and we wait - ed on the thun - der,

wait - ed on the thun - der. _____

Operator
(That's Not the Way It Feels)
Words and Music by Jim Croce

Tangled Up in Blue

Words and Music by Bob Dylan

1. Ear - ly one morn - in' the sun ___ was shin - in',
3., 5., 7. *See additional lyrics*

I was layin' in bed, won - d'rin' if ___ she'd changed at all, ___ if her

hair was ___ still red. Her folks, they said our lives ___ to - geth - er

sure was gon - na be rough. They nev - er did like ___ Ma - ma's home - made dress, ___ Pa - pa's

bank book was - n't big e - nough. And I was stand - in' on the side of the road, ___ rain ___

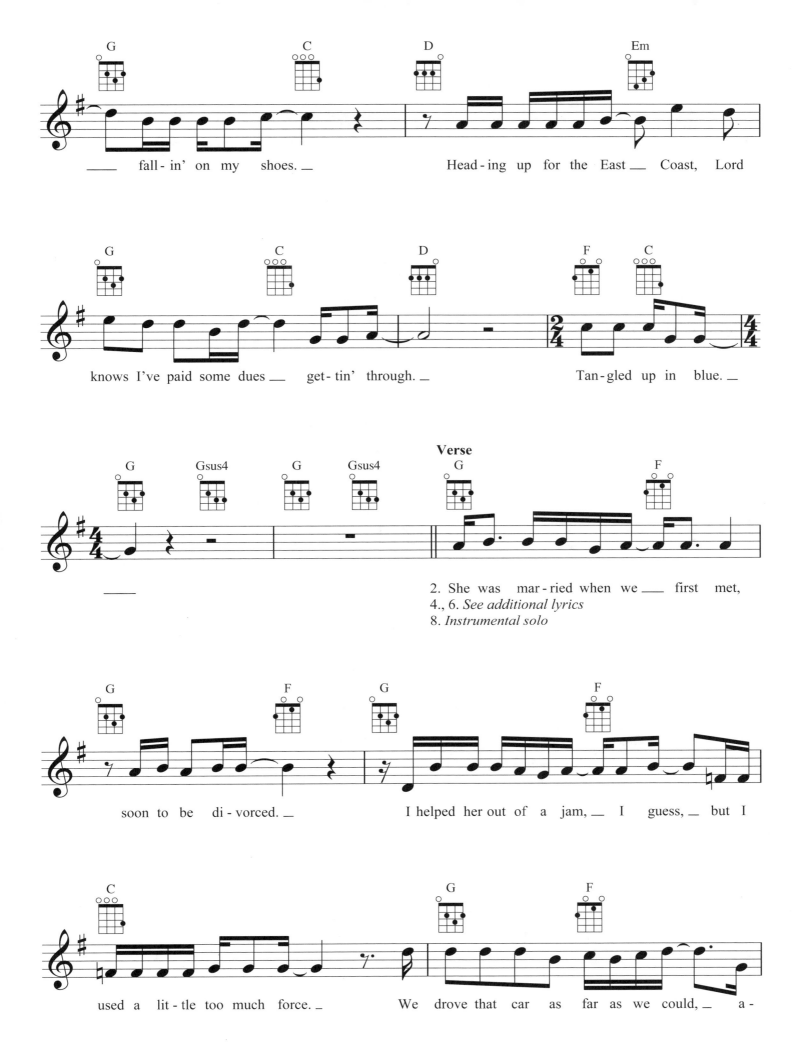

_____ fall-in' on my shoes. _____   Head-ing up for the East _____ Coast, Lord

knows I've paid some dues _____ get-tin' through. _____   Tan-gled up in blue. _____

Verse

_____

2. She was mar-ried when we _____ first met,
4., 6. *See additional lyrics*
8. *Instrumental solo*

soon to be di-vorced. _____   I helped her out of a jam, _____ I guess, _____ but I

used a lit-tle too much force. _____   We drove that car as far as we could, _____ a-

ban - doned it ___ out West, ___ split up ___ on a dark, ___ sad night, ___ both a -

gree - ing it ___ was best. ___ As she turned a - round to look at me ___ as I ___

___ was a walk - in' a - way, ___ I heard her say o - ver my ___ shoul - der, ___ "We'll meet ___

___ a - gain ___ some - day ___ on the av - e - nue." ___

Tan - gled up in blue. ___

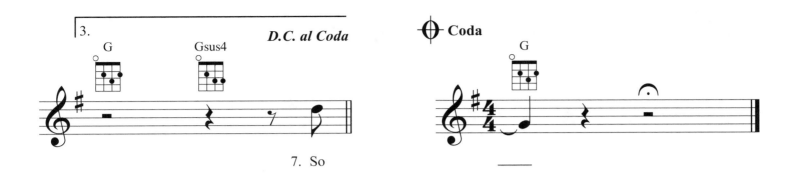

Additional Lyrics

3. I had a job in the great north woods,
   Working as a cook for a spell.
   But I never did like it all that much
   And one day the axe just fell.
   So I drifted down to New Orleans
   Where I was lucky to be employed.
   Workin' for a while on a fishin' boat
   Right outside of Delacroix.
   But all the while I was alone,
   The past was close behind.
   I seen a lot of women,
   But she never escaped my mind, and I just grew
   Tangled up in blue.

4. She was workin' in a topless place
   And I stopped in for a beer.
   I just kept lookin' at the side of her face
   In the spotlight so clear.
   And later on when the crowd thinned out,
   I's just about to do the same.
   She was standin' there in back of my chair,
   Said to me, "Don't I know your name?"
   I muttered somethin' underneath my breath,
   She studied the lines on my face.
   I must admit I felt a little uneasy
   When she bent down to tie the laces of my shoe.
   Tangled up in blue.

5. She lit a burner on the stove and offered me a pipe.
   "I thought you'd never say hello," she said.
   "You look like the silent type."
   Then she opened up a book of poems
   And handed it to me,
   Written by an Italian poet
   From the thirteenth century.
   And ev'ry one of them words rang true
   And glowed like burnin' coal,
   Pourin' off of ev'ry page
   Like it was written in my soul from me to you.
   Tangled up in blue.

6. I lived with them on Montague Street
   In a basement down the stairs.
   There was music in the cafés at night
   And revolution in the air.
   Then he started into dealing with slaves
   And something inside of him died.
   She had to sell ev'rything she owned
   And froze up inside.
   And when it finally, the bottom fell out
   I became withdrawn.
   The only thing I knew how to do
   Was to keep on keepin' on like a bird that flew.
   Tangled up in blue.

7. So now I'm goin' back again,
   I got to get to her somehow.
   All the people we used to know,
   They're an illusion to me now.
   Some are mathematicians;
   Some are carpenters' wives.
   Don't know how it all got started,
   I don't know what they're doin' with their lives.
   But me, I'm still on the road,
   Headin' for another joint.
   We always did feel the same,
   We just saw it from a diff'rent point of view.
   Tangled up in blue.

Time for Me to Fly

Words and Music by Kevin Cronin

Outro

Time for me ___ to fly. _____ I've got to set ___

___ my - self free. Time for me ___ to fly. _____

That's just how it's got to ___ be. _____

I know it hurts to say ___ good - bye, ___ but it's

time for me ___ to fly. _____ It's

time for me ___ to fly. _____

Into the Mystic

Words and Music by Van Morrison

Let your soul and spir - it fly _____ in - to the mys - tic.

Pre-Chorus

And when that fog - horn blows, _____ I will be

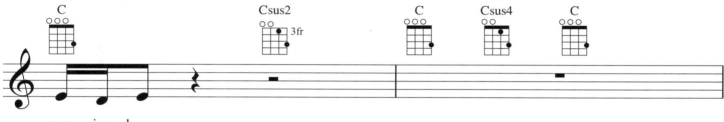

com - ing home.

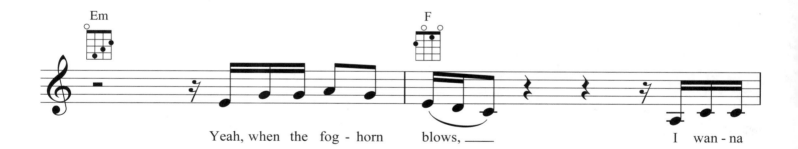

Yeah, when the fog - horn blows, _____ I wan - na

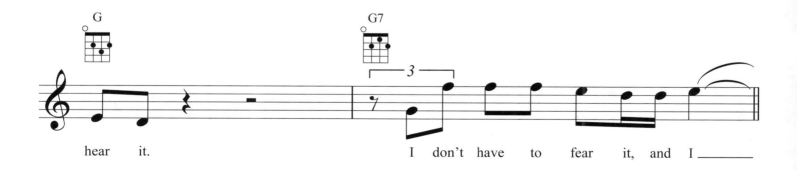

hear it. I don't have to fear it, and I _____

Who'll Stop the Rain

Words and Music by John Fogerty

Wish You Were Here

Words and Music by Roger Waters and David Gilmour

Chorus

Did they get you to trade ____ your he - roes for ghosts, ____ hot ash - es for trees, ____ hot air ____ for a cool ____ breeze, ____ cold ___ com - fort for charge? ____ And did you ____ ex - change ____ a walk - on part ____ in the war ____ for a lead ____ role in a cage? ____ *(Instrumental)*

Interlude

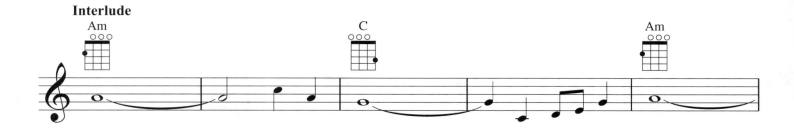

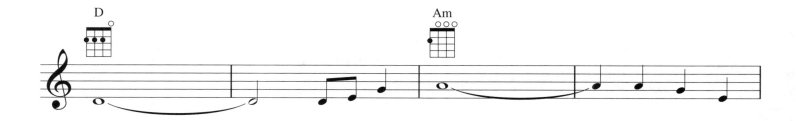

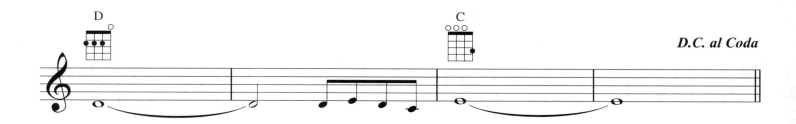

D.C. al Coda

Wish you _____ were here. _____

Additional Lyrics

2. How I wish, how I wish you were here.
   We're just two lost souls swimming in a fish bowl year after year.
   Running over the same old ground, what have we found?
   The same old fears. Wish you were here.

Vincent
(Starry Starry Night)

Words and Music by Don McLean

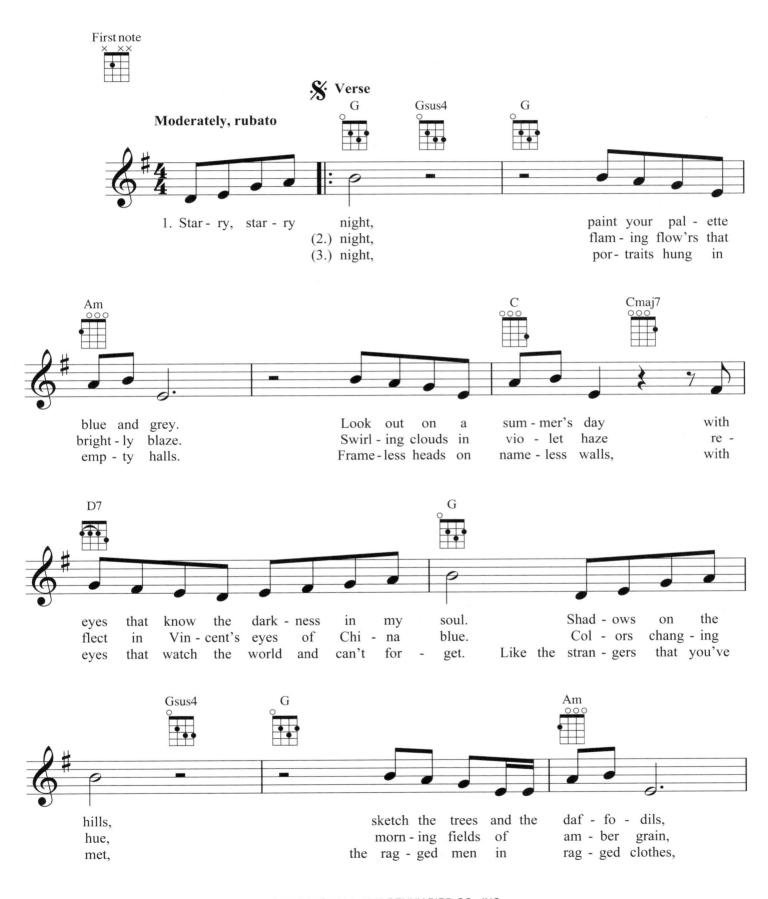

catch the breeze and the win - ter chills
weath - ered fac - es lined in pain
the sil - ver thorn of blood - y rose,

col - ors on the snow - y lin - en land.
soothed be - neath the art - ist's lov - ing hand.
crushed and bro - ken on the vir - gin snow.

in
are
lie

Now I un - der -
Now I un - der -
Now I think I

Chorus

stand
stand
know

what you tried to say to me,
what you tried to say to me,
what you tried to say to me,

how you suf - fered for your san - i - ty,
how you suf - fered for your san - i - ty,
how you suf - fered for your san - i - ty,

how you tried to set them
how you tried to set them
how you tried to set them

To Coda

free. They would not lis - ten; they did not know how. ___
free. They would not lis - ten; they did not know how. ___
free. They would not lis - ten; they're not

Per - haps they'll lis - ten
Per - haps they'll lis - ten

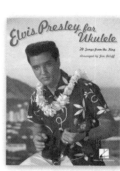

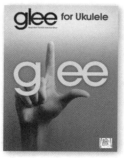